# At Christmas Be Merry

## Verses Selected and Illustrated by P. K. Roche

VIKING KESTREL

JE 394
A

VIKING KESTREL

Viking Penguin Inc., 40 West 23rd Street, New York, New York 10010, U.S.A.
Penguin Books Ltd, Harmondsworth, Middlesex, England
Penguin Books Australia Ltd, Ringwood, Victoria, Australia
Penguin Books Canada Limited, 2801 John Street, Markham, Ontario, Canada L3R 1B4
Penguin Books (N.Z.) Ltd, 182–190 Wairau Road, Auckland 10, New Zealand

First published in 1986 by Viking Penguin Inc.
Published simultaneously in Canada
Printed in Japan by Dai Nippon Printing Co., Ltd.
Set in Granjon
1  2  3  4  5  90  89  88  87  86

Library of Congress catalog card number: 84-21917     ISBN 0-670-80421-5

## CONTENTS

Grateful acknowledgment is made to the following for permission to reprint
copyrighted material:
Valerie Worth Bahlke: "Christmas Ornaments," copyright © 1976 by Valerie Worth
Bahlke.     Clarion Books/Ticknor & Fields, a Houghton-Mifflin Company:
"I want to keep" from *A Bunch of Poems and Verses* by Beatrice Schenk de Regniers.
Copyright © 1977 by Beatrice Schenk de Regniers.     Grosset & Dunlap, Inc.:
"When Grandmama Was Young" from *The Sparrow Bush* by Elizabeth Coatsworth,
copyright © 1966 by Grosset & Dunlap, Inc.     Harper & Row, Publishers, Inc.:
"People Buy a Lot of Things" from *For Days and Days* by Annette Wynne
(J. B. Lippincott), copyright 1919 by Harper & Row, Publishers Inc. Renewed 1947 by
Annette Wynne; "At Christmas Time" from *In One Door and Out the Other* by Aileen
Fisher (Thomas Y. Crowell), copyright © 1969 by Aileen Fisher; "Do Not Open Until
Christmas" from *Counting the Days* by James S. Tippett, copyright 1940 by Harper
& Row, Publishers, Inc.     Harper & Row, Publishers, Inc., and Harold Ober
Associates Inc.: five stanzas from "In the Week When Christmas Comes" and one
stanza from "Now Every Child" from *Eleanor Farjeon's Poems for Children*. Copyright
1927, 1953 by Eleanor Farjeon.     Harper & Row Publishers, Inc., and World's
Work Ltd: "A City Street at Christmas" from *Crickety Cricket* by James S. Tippett.
Copyright 1940 by Harper & Row, Publishers, Inc.     Liveright Publishing
Corporation and Grafton Books, a Division of the Collins Publishing Group: The
lines from "little tree" from *Tulips & Chimneys* by e. e. cummings are reprinted by
permission of Liveright Publishing Corporation. Copyright 1923, 1925, and renewed
1951, 1953 by e. e. cummings. Copyright © 1973, 1976 by the Trustees for the e. e.
cummings Trust. Copyright © 1973, 1976 by George James Firmage. "little tree" from
*The Complete Poems 1913–1962* by e. e. cummings published by Grafton Books, a
Division of the Collins Publishing Group.     Macmillan Publishing Company:
"Great-Uncle Willie" from *Poems* by Rachel Field (New York: Macmillan, 1957).
Barbara Pilon: "Fir Tree Tall" by Joan Hanson from *Concrete Is Not Always Hard*,
edited by Barbara Pilon (Middletown, CT: Xerox Education Publications, 1972).
G. P. Putnam's Sons: "Waiting" from *Hop, Skip and Jump!* by Dorothy Aldis,
copyright 1934, copyright renewed © 1961 by Dorothy Aldis.
Yale University Press: "Bundles" from *Songs for Parents* by John Farrar.

*For my editor and friend, Regina Hayes*

At Christmas be merry, and thankful withal,
And feast thy poor neighbors, the great with the small.

# Christmas Week

This is the week when Christmas comes.

Let every pudding burst with plums,
And every tree bear dolls and drums,
In the week when Christmas comes.

Let every hall have boughs of green,
With berries glowing in between,
In the week when Christmas comes.

Let every steeple ring a bell
With a joyful tale to tell,
In the week when Christmas comes.

This is the week when Christmas comes.

All along
The city street
Busy Christmas shoppers
Meet.

I like walking there
Because
I can talk
With Santa Claus,

And at windows
Make long stops,
Or gaze into
The candy shops.

We walk along
On many nights
To see the show
Of Christmas lights.

Get ready your money and come to me,
I sell a young lamb for one penny.
Young lambs to sell! Young lambs to sell!
If I'd as much money as I could tell,
I never would cry, Young lambs to sell!

A bundle is a funny thing,
It always sets me wondering;
For whether it is thin or wide
You never know just what's inside.

Especially on Christmas week,
Temptation is so great to peek!
Now wouldn't it be much more fun
If shoppers carried things undone!

People buy a lot of things—
Carts and balls and nails and rings,
But I would buy a bird that sings.

Christmas is coming,
  The geese are getting fat,
Please to put a penny
  In the old man's hat.
If you haven't got a penny,
  A ha'penny will do;
If you haven't got a ha'penny,
  Then God bless you!

In every house on every street
around and up and down
there's something special going on,
in every house in town:

Gifts to make
and lights to string
and sweets to bake
and bells to ring
(with snowflakes sifting down),
and shiny eyes
and dancy feet
in every house on every street,
on every street in town.

11

# Christmas Eve

Ride away, ride away,
   Johnny shall ride,
He shall have a pussy cat
   Tied to one side;
He shall have a little dog
   Tied to the other,
And Johnny shall ride
   To see his grandmother.

The boxes break
At the corners,
Their sides
Sink weak;

They are tied up
Every year
With the same
Gray string;

But under the split
Lids, a fortune
Shines: globes
Of gold and sapphire,

Silver spires and
Bells, jeweled
Nightingales with
Pearly tails.

Fir
tree tall
Lights glittering
Bright tinsel hung
Shimmering, glimmering
Laughter shining in the eyes
of boys
and girls
Lovely lovely
Christmas tree.

little tree
little silent Christmas tree
you are so little
you are more like a flower

Villagers all, this frosty tide,
Let your doors swing open wide,
Though wind may follow, and snow beside,
Yet draw us in by your fire to bide;
  Joy shall be yours in the morning!

Here we stand in the cold and the sleet,
Blowing fingers and stamping feet,
Come from far away you to greet—
You by the fire and we in the street—
  Bidding you joy in the morning!

Jeremiah, blow the fire,
Puff, puff, puff!
First you blow it gently
Then you blow it rough.

We've hung our Christmas stockings.
They look so long and thin
And now we're waiting in our beds
For morning to begin.

It's black outside the window.
It rattles at the door.
Oh, will Tomorrow ever come!
Or won't it any more!

On a winter night
When the moon is low
The rabbits hop on the frozen snow.
The woodpecker sleeps in his hole in the tree
And fast asleep is the chickadee.
Twelve o'clock
And the world is still
As the Christmas star comes over the hill
The angels sing, and sing again:
"Peace on earth, goodwill to men."

# Christmas Day

The dark night wakes, the glory breaks,
And Christmas comes once more.

I shake-shake,
Shake-shake,
Shake the package well.

But what there is
Inside of it,
Shaking will not tell.

23

Now every Child that dwells on earth,
Stand up, stand up and sing!
The passing night has given birth
Unto the Children's King.
Sing sweet as the flute,
Sing clear as the horn,
Sing joy of the Children
Come Christmas the morn!
Little Christ Jesus
Our Brother is born.

High on our dining-room wall,
Smiling and little and neat,
For years Great-Uncle Willie
Has watched us sit and eat.
Breakfast, dinner, supper,
Parties and afternoon tea—
I can't help thinking sometimes
How hungry he must be!

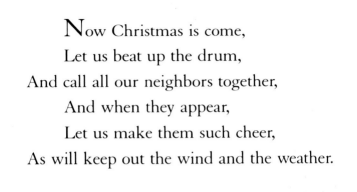

Now Christmas is come,
Let us beat up the drum,
And call all our neighbors together,
And when they appear,
Let us make them such cheer,
As will keep out the wind and the weather.

Jingle bells! jingle, bells!
  Jingle all the way;
Oh, what fun it is to ride
  In a one-horse open sleigh.

Little Jack Horner
Sat in the corner,
Eating a Christmas pie;
He put in his thumb,
And pulled out a plum,
And said, What a good boy am I!

Jack be nimble,
Jack be quick,
Jack jump over
The candlestick.

Mary had a pretty bird,
Feathers bright and yellow,
Slender legs—upon my word
He was a pretty fellow!

Once upon a time
When Grandmama was young,
Foxes played on bagpipes,
Raccoons beat on drums,

Mice danced minuets,
Squirrels two-stepped gaily,
And the unmarried cottontails
Gave tea parties daily.

I want to keep
from falling asleep.
I want to be waking
and listen to talking
around me buzz buzz.

Buzz buzz
all around.
What a buzz buzzy
sound
buzz zuzz
zzzzzz z z z z
zzzz

32